MENDELSSOHN
Masterpieces for Solo Piano
25 Works

Edited by
Julius Rietz

From Breitkopf & Härtel's Complete Works Edition

DOVER PUBLICATIONS, INC.
Mineola, New York

Copyright

Copyright © 2000 by Dover Publications, Inc.
All rights reserved under Pan American and International Copyright Conventions.

Published in Canada by General Publishing Company, Ltd., 30 Lesmill Road, Don Mills, Toronto, Ontario.

Bibliographical Note

This Dover edition, first published in 2000, is a new compilation of piano works drawn from Series 11, "Für Pianoforte allein," of *Felix Mendelssohn Bartholdy's Werke. Kritisch durchgesehene Ausgabe von Julius Rietz. Mit Genehmigung der Originalverleger*, originally published by Breitkopf & Härtel, Leipzig, n.d. [1874–77].

International Standard Book Number: 0-486-41161-4

Manufactured in the United States of America
Dover Publications, Inc., 31 East 2nd Street, Mineola, N.Y. 11501

Contents

"Light and airy": Character piece in E major (Op. 7, No. 7)   2

Rondo capriccioso in E major (Op. 14)   8

Three Fantasies (Caprices) (Op. 16)
    Fantasy in A minor   16
    Scherzo in E minor   19
    Fantasy in E major   22

Fantasy in F-sharp minor (Op. 28)   26

Scherzo in B minor   40

Scherzo a capriccio in F-sharp minor   42

Prelude and Fugue in E minor (Op. 35, No. 1)   50

Variations sérieuses in D minor (Op. 54)   59

Songs without Words
    Song without Words (Op. 19, No. 5)   72
    Venetian Gondola Song in F-sharp minor (Op. 30, No. 6)   76
    Folk Song (Op. 53, No. 5)   78
    Spring Song (Op. 62, No. 6)   81
    Venetian Gondola Song in A minor (Op. 62, No. 5)   84
    Spinning Song (Op. 67, No. 4)   86
    Albumleaf in E minor (Op. 117)   90

Pieces for children (Op. 72)
    1. Allegro non troppo   96
    2. Andante sostenuto   97
    3. Allegretto   98
    4. Andante con moto   99
    5. Allegro assai   100
    6. Vivace   102

Sonata in G minor (Op. 105)
    I. Allegro   104
    II. Adagio   110
    III. Presto   113

Perpetuum mobile (Op. 119)   118

MENDELSSOHN
Masterpieces for Solo Piano
25 Works

To Ludwig Berger

"Light and airy"
No. 7 of *Seven character pieces*
"Leicht und luftig" from *Sieben Charakterstücke*, Op. 7 (1827)

Presto.

sempre staccato e **pp**

sempre **pp**

"Light and airy" / 3

4 / "Light and airy"

"Light and airy" / 5

6 / "Light and airy"

"Light and airy" / 7

Rondo capriccioso in E major
Op. 14 (1824)

Rondo capriccioso / 9

10 / Rondo capriccioso

Rondo capriccioso / 11

12 / Rondo capriccioso

Rondo capriccioso / 13

14 / Rondo capriccioso

Rondo capriccioso / 15

THREE FANTASIES OR CAPRICES
Drei Phantasien oder Capricen, Op. 16 (1829)

To Ann Taylor

Fantasy in A minor
Op. 16, No. 1

p
cresc.
ff
dim.
p
pp
pp
poco riten.
a tempo
p
p
cresc.
sf
cresc.
ff
p
p
cresc.
sf
sempre cresc.
ff
p
espress.
cresc.
f
p
con fuoco
cresc.
p
cresc.
f
con fuoco
f
sf

18 / Fantasy in A minor

To Honoria Taylor

Scherzo in E minor
Op. 16, No. 2

20 / Scherzo in E minor

Scherzo in E minor / 21

To Susan Taylor

Fantasy in E major
Op. 16, No. 3

Andante.

Fantasy in E major / 23

24 / Fantasy in E major

Fantasy in E major / 25

To Ignaz Moscheles

Fantasy in F-sharp minor

Phantasie: "Sonate écossaise," Op. 28 (1833)

Fantasy in F-sharp minor / 27

28 / Fantasy in F-sharp minor

Andante tempo I.

Fantasy in F-sharp minor / 29

30 / Fantasy in F-sharp minor

Fantasy in F-sharp minor / 31

32 / Fantasy in F-sharp minor

Fantasy in F-sharp minor

34 / Fantasy in F-sharp minor

Fantasy in F-sharp minor / 35

36 / Fantasy in F-sharp minor

Fantasy in F-sharp minor / 37

38 / Fantasy in F-sharp minor

Fantasy in F-sharp minor / 39

Scherzo in B minor
(after 1828)

Prestissimo.

Scherzo in B minor / 41

Scherzo a capriccio in F-sharp minor
(before 1833)

Presto scherzando.

Scherzo a capriccio / 43

sempre stacc.
cresc.
cresc.
f
cresc.
sf
f
sf
sf
sf
sf
sf
sf
con fuoco
sf
sf
sf
dim.
sf
sf
sf
sf
cresc.
f

Scherzo a capriccio / 45

46 / Scherzo a capriccio

Scherzo a capriccio / 47

48 / Scherzo a capriccio

Scherzo a capriccio / 49

Prelude and Fugue in E minor

No. 1 of *Six Preludes and Fugues*, Op. 35

(Prelude, 1837 / Fugue, 1827)

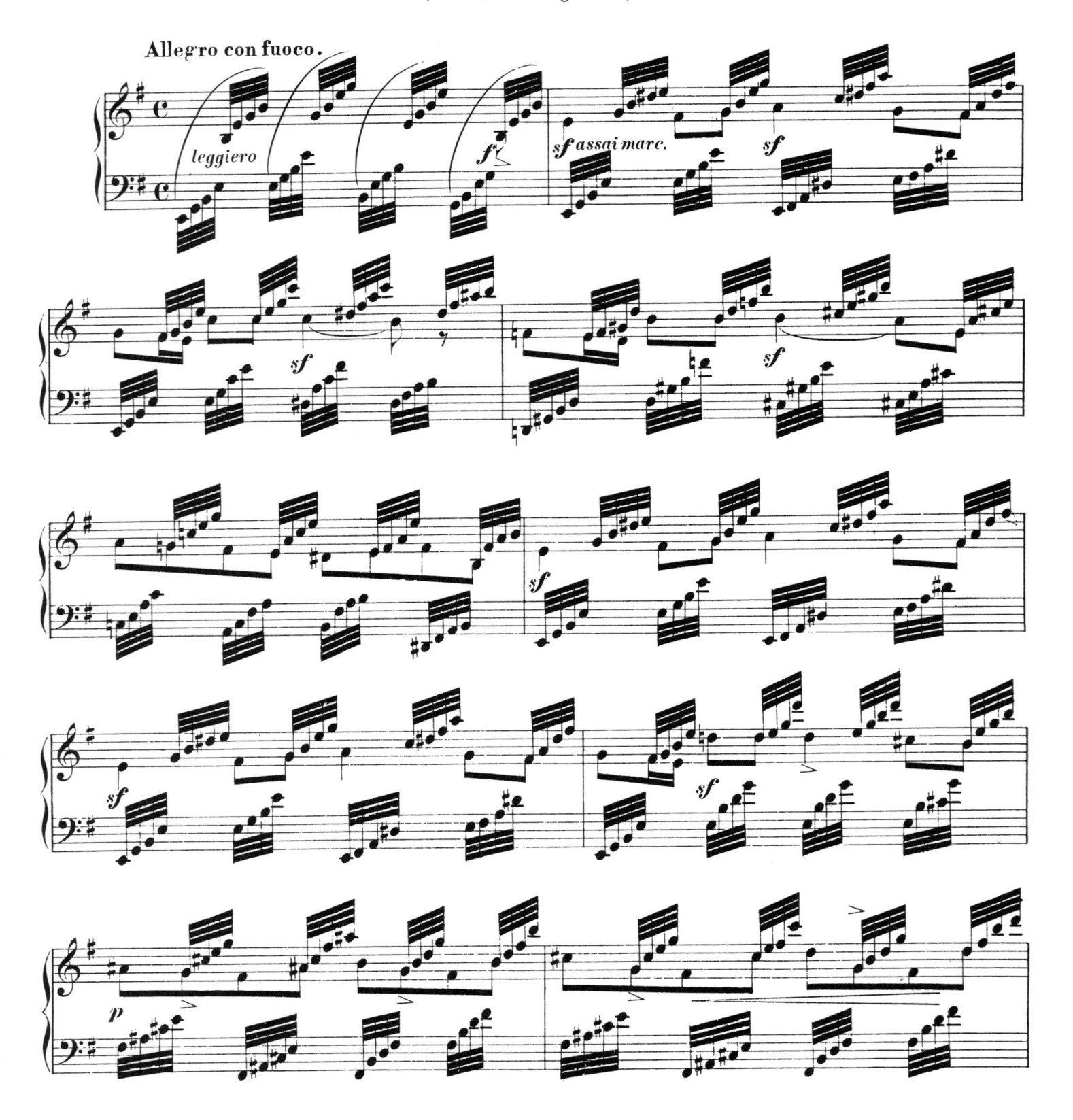

Prelude and Fugue / 51

52 / Prelude and Fugue

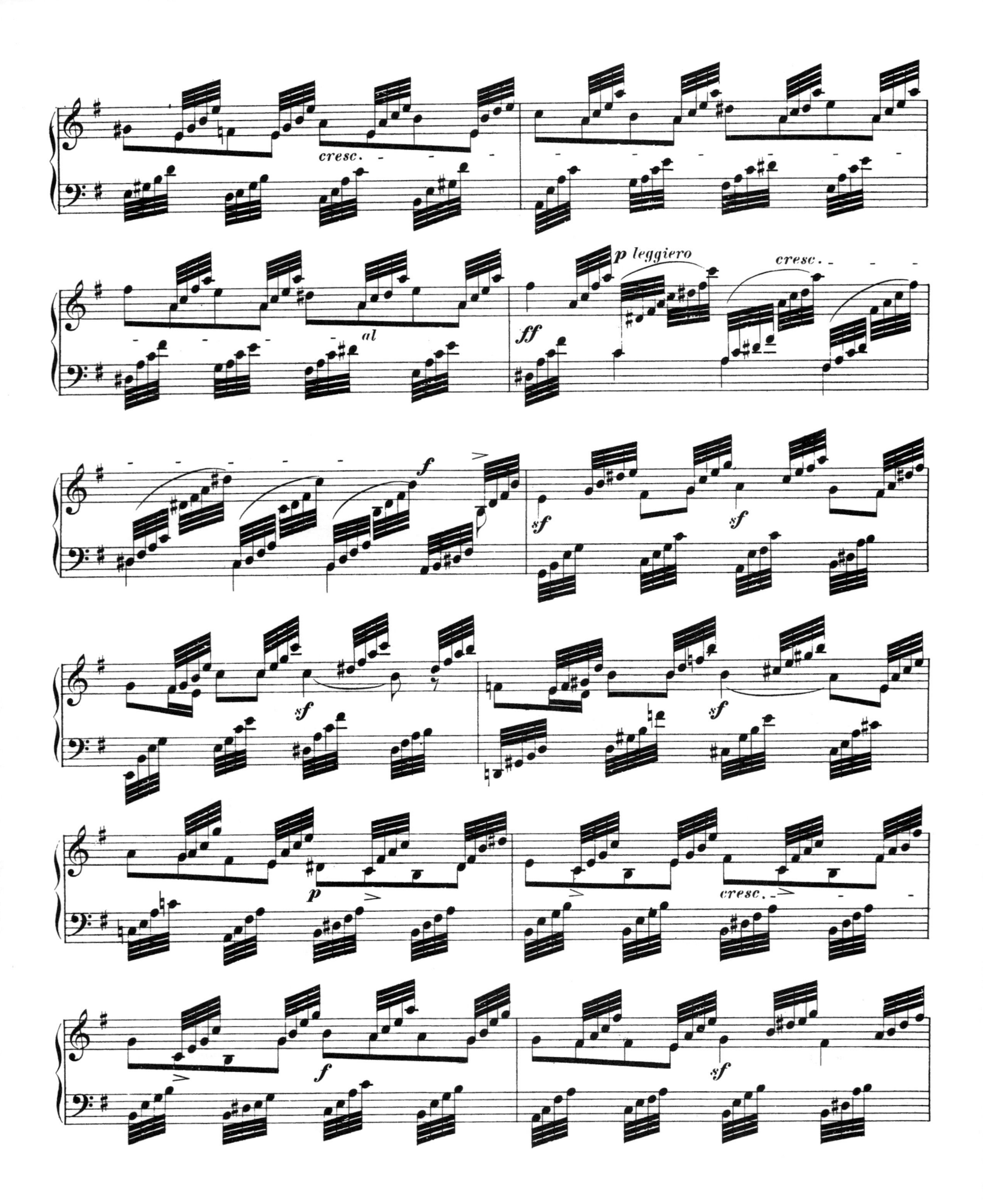

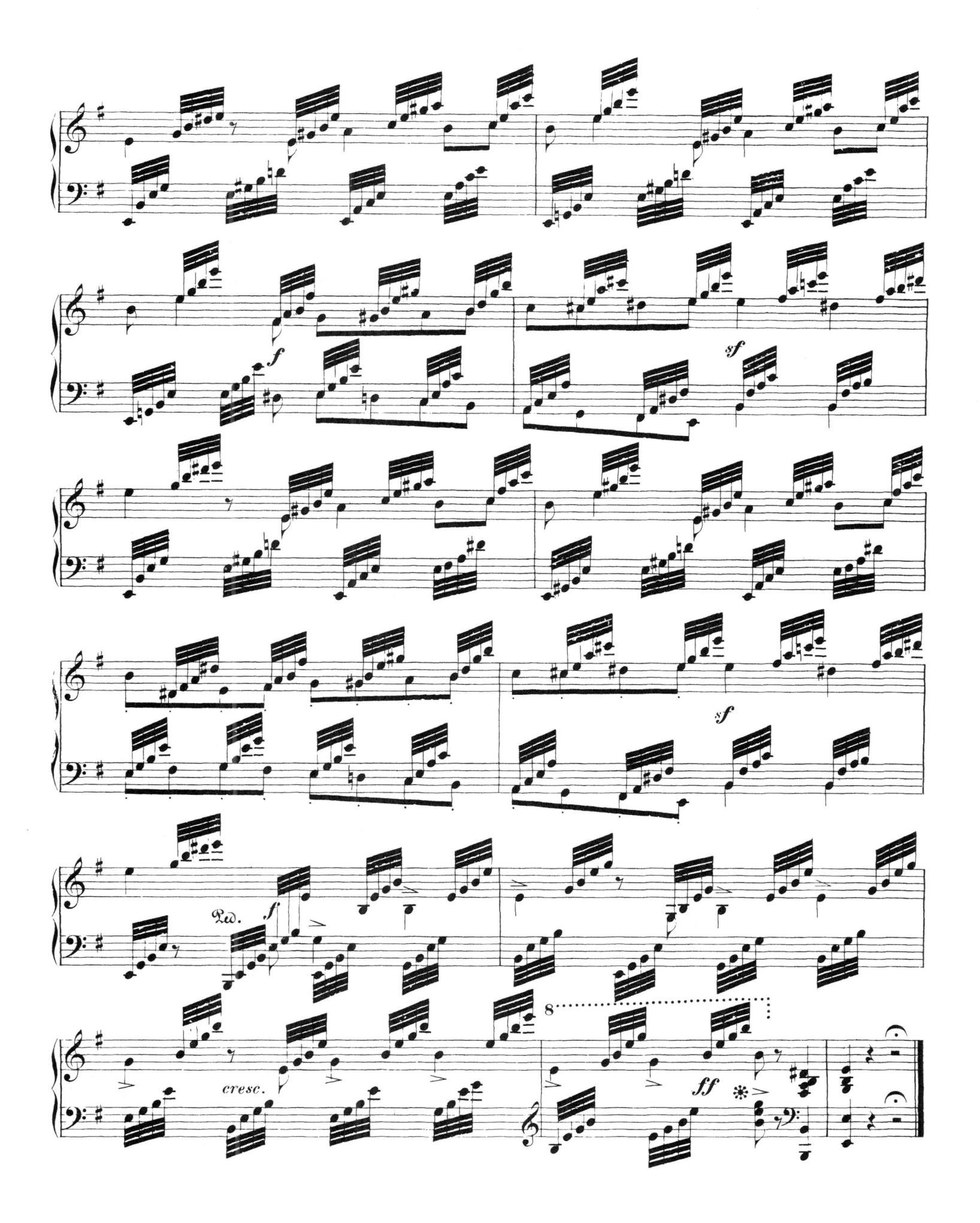

Prelude and Fugue / 53

Fuga

Andante espressivo.

Prelude and Fugue / 55

56 / Prelude and Fugue

Prelude and Fugue / 57

58 / Prelude and Fugue

Variations sérieuses in D minor
Op. 54 (1841)

Var. 3.
Più animato.

60 / Variations sérieuses

Variations sérieuses / 61

62 / Variations sérieuses

Variations sérieuses / 63

Var. 10.
Moderato.

Var. 11.
cantabile

Var. 12.
Tempo di Tema.

Variations sérieuses / 65

Var. 13.
sempre assai leggiero

sf sempre assai marcato

66 / Variations sérieuses

Var. 14. Adagio.
mf
p
cresc.
f
dim.
ritard.
3
p
Var. 15.
poco a poco più agitato
sempre pp
cresc.
cresc.
sf
dim.
Var. 16.
Allegro vivace.
6
p
cresc.
f
p
cresc.
sf
sf
sf
sf
sf

Var. 17.

68 / Variations sérieuses

Variations sérieuses / 69

70 / Variations sérieuses

Songs without Words

Seven pieces
from Opp. 19, 30, 53, 62, 67 and 117

Song without Words

No. 5 in F-sharp minor, from *Lieder ohne Worte*, Book I, Op. 19 (1829–30)

Poco agitato.

Song without Words (Op. 19/5)

74 / Song without Words (Op. 19/5)

Song without Words (Op. 19/5) / 75

To Elisa von Woringen

Venetian Gondola Song
"Venetianisches Gondellied"
No. 6 in F-sharp minor, from *Lieder ohne Worte*, Book II, Op. 30 (1833–34)

Allegretto tranquillo.

Venetian Gondola Song (F-sharp minor)

To Sophie Horsley

Folk Song
"Volkslied"
No. 5 in A minor, from *Lieder ohne Worte*, Book IV, Op. 53 (1839–41)

Folk Song / 79

80 / Folk Song

Spring Song

"Frühlingslied"
No. 6 in A major, from *Lieder ohne Worte*, Book V, Op. 62 (1842–44)

Allegretto grazioso.

82 / Spring Song

Spring Song / 83

To Clara Schumann

Venetian Gondola Song

"Venetianisches Gondellied"
No. 5 in A minor, from *Lieder ohne Worte*, Book V, Op. 62 (1842–44)

Venetian Gondola Song (A minor)

Spinning Song
"Spinnerlied"
No. 4 in C major, from *Lieder ohne Worte*, Book VI, Op. 67 (1843–45)

Spinning Song / 87

88 / Spinning Song

Spinning Song / 89

Albumleaf
(Song without Words)

"Albumblatt" (Lied ohne Worte) in E minor
Op. 117 (1837?)

Albumleaf / 91

92 / Albumleaf

Albumleaf / 93

94 / Albumleaf

Albumleaf / 95

No. 1: *To Lilli Benecke* / No. 3: *To Eduard Benecke*

Pieces for children
[6] *Kinderstücke*, Op. 72 (1842)

Allegro non troppo. **1.**

2.

Andante sostenuto.

3.

Allegretto.

4.

Andante con moto.

5.

Allegro assai.

Pieces for children / 101

6.

Pieces for children / 103

Sonata in G minor
Op. 105 (1821)

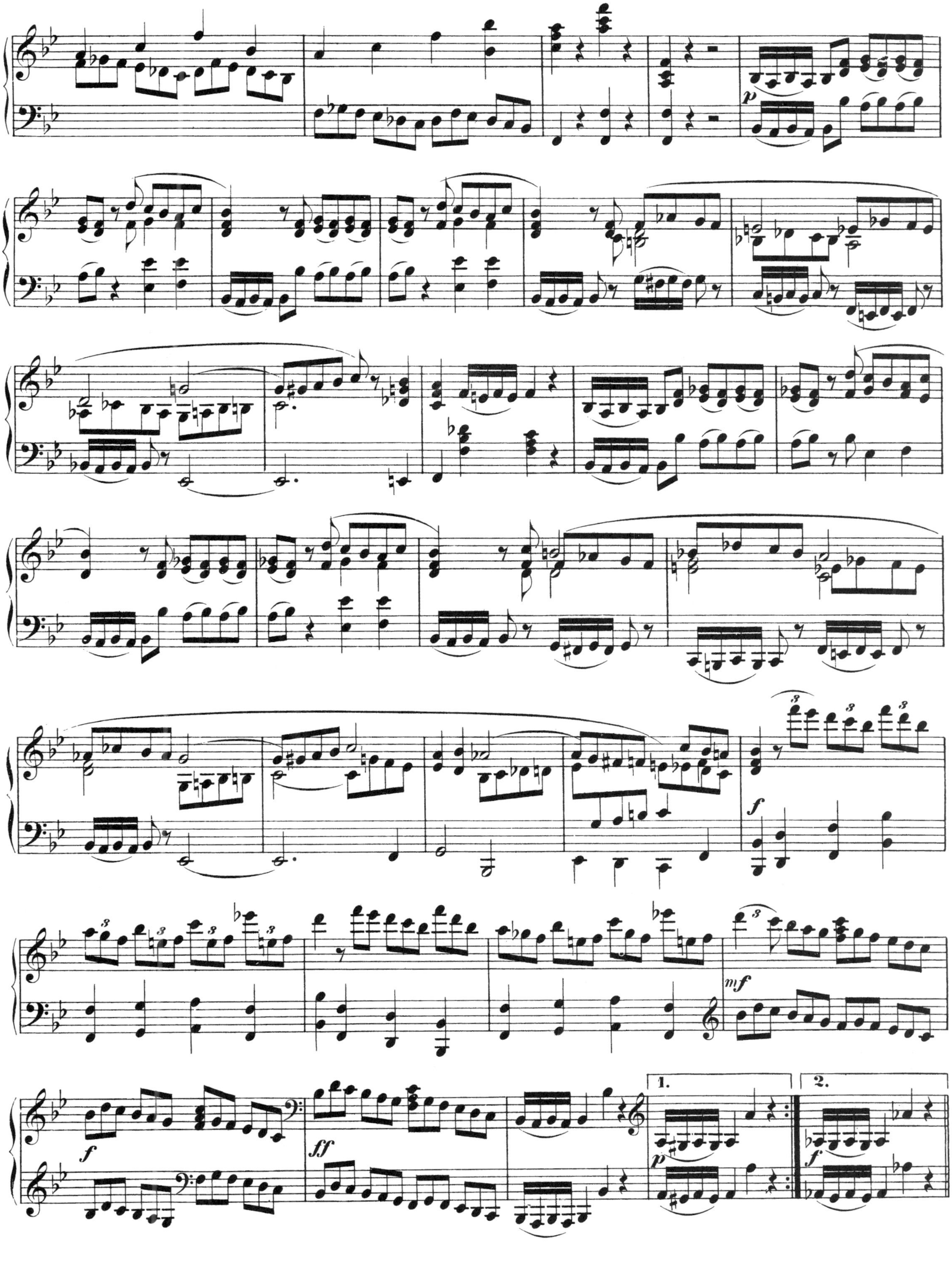
1.
2.

Sonata in G minor

Sonata in G minor / 107

108 / Sonata in G minor

Sonata in G minor / 109

110 / Sonata in G minor

Sonata in G minor / 111

112 / Sonata in G minor

Sonata in G minor / 113

114 / Sonata in G minor

Sonata in G minor / 115

116 / Sonata in G minor

Sonata in G minor / 117

Perpetuum mobile
Op. 119 (1873)

Prestissimo.

Perpetuum mobile / 119

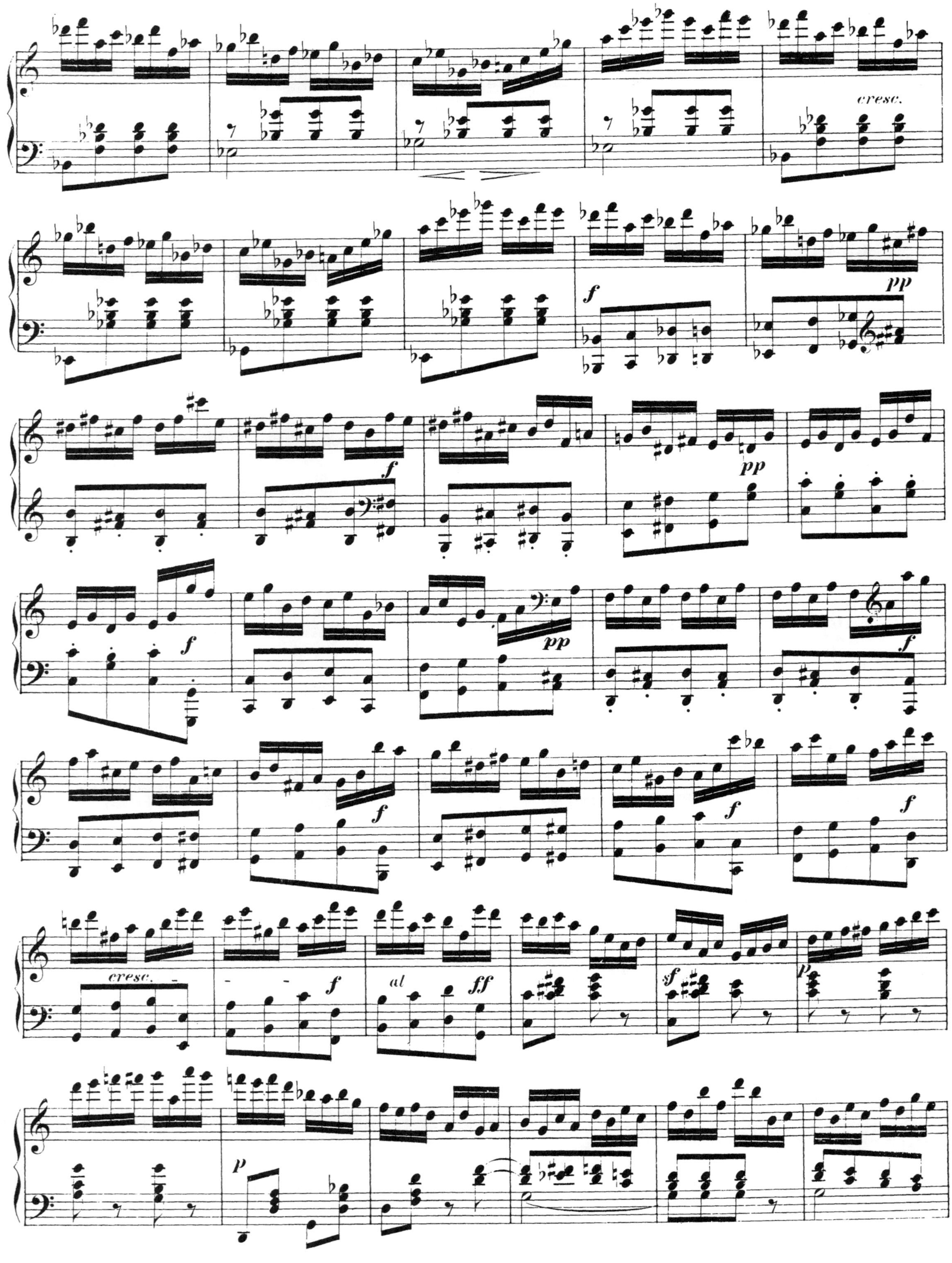
cresc.
f
pp
f
pp
f
pp
f
f
f
f
f
cresc.
f
al
ff
sf
p
p

Perpetuum mobile / 121

122 / Perpetuum mobile

END OF EDITION